BRANDING:

CRAFTING A LASTING IDENTITY FOR YOUR HANDMADE BUSINESS

Madison E. Bonham

TABLE OF CONTENTS

INTRODUCTION

Welcome to the world of 'Branding: Crafting a Lasting Identity for Your Handmade Business.' You'll set out on a journey to learn the art and science of branding in this book, which is designed especially for the special world of handmade enterprises. Discover the techniques for developing a unique identity that not only distinguishes your works but also tells a compelling story to your audience. This book is your guide to developing your handcrafted passion into a recognizable and successful business, from creating attractive logos to crafting fascinating tales.

Madison.

CHAPTER 1

WHAT IS BRANDING

The strategic process of developing and establishing a distinctive and identifiable identity for a product, service, or business is known as **BRANDING**. It entails using numerous components, including the logo, design, message, and customer experience, to create a unified and consistent image. Successful branding strives to set the brand apart from rivals, communicate its values, gain the confidence of customers, and elicit certain feelings or connections. It is essential for shaping consumer views, fostering customer loyalty, and ultimately affecting a company's marketability. Branding is also the Process of

Creating a unique Identity and image for a Product, Service or Company.

Importance of Branding for Handmade Business

Branding does a lot of things to business and some of the reasons for branding are:

<u>Distinguishing Features</u>

Branding makes your handcrafted products stand out in a market where there may be many comparable things. It offers your company a distinctive personality that distinguishes it from rivals and enables buyers to remember and recognize your goods.

Perceived Value

Strong branding raises the estimation of the worth of your handcrafted goods. Customers frequently pay more for a company that has a strong brand because they believe it to be high-quality, handcrafted, and distinctive.

Credibility and Trustworthiness

Customers are more likely to trust and believe in a business that projects a consistent, polished image. Customers are more inclined to trust the caliber and authenticity of your handcrafted goods when you have a strong brand.

Storytelling

Handmade business owners frequently have a personal history or a love for what they do. With the help of branding, you can tell your consumers this narrative and establish an emotional connection with them that will inspire loyalty.

Recognition

Branding makes your business and items more recognizable to consumers. They can easily connect your brand or packaging with your distinctive goods when they see it, which makes it simpler for them to pick your products again in the future.

Consistency

A unified and expert image is created through consistent branding across all touchpoints, from product packaging to social media. Customers are reassured and given a feeling of dependability by this constancy.

Market Positioning

Branding enables you to place your handcrafted company in a certain market niche or sector. You may target a certain demographic and explain why your items are the greatest choice for their requirements.

Recurring Business and Loyalty

Strong branding encourages client loyalty. Customers are more likely to return and spread the word about your handcrafted goods when they have a pleasant brand experience.

Expansion Possibilities

Your brand may develop into additional product lines or joint ventures as your handcrafted business develops.

Since buyers already trust your brand, it is simpler to launch new products with a strong brand.

<u>Marketing Efforts</u>

Building your brand lays the groundwork for your marketing initiatives. Your messaging, images, and entire markcting plan will have a clear direction thanks to it, which will increase the effectiveness of your promotional efforts.

Defining Your Brand Essence

Defining a brand essence entails narrowing down the essential beliefs, character traits, and distinctive features that define your company. Here are some easy steps to help you identify the essence of your brand:

1. ***Determine Core Values:*** Discover the guiding

principles behind your brand. What values and beliefs

inform your choices and actions?

2. ***Recognize Your Audience***: Who Are Your Target

Clients? What are they concerned with? Your brand's

essence need to be felt by them.

3. ***Examine Differentiators:*** What distinguishes your

brand from rivals? Determine the traits and unique

selling features you possess.

4. ***Create a Brand Promise***: Create a succinct

declaration that encompasses the commitments your

brand makes to customers.

5. *Capture Character:* Think of your brand as a person and describe it that way. Is it personable, creative, competent, etc.?

6. *Visualize Your Brand's Image*: Picture your brand as a person, a location, or an item. You can see the essence of it by doing this.

7. *Appeal to Emotion:* Think about the feelings you want your brand to arouse in consumers. How ought they to feel when they deal with your brand?

8. *Keep It Simple*: Condense your brand's essence into a succinct, resonant sentence that expresses your brand's core values.

9. *Consistency*: Once your brand essence has been established, make sure it is consistently expressed in all of your brand's elements, from images to message.

Remember that your brand's essence is the basis of its identity and should direct all of your company's interactions, messages, and activities.

CHAPTER 2

5 BASIC ELEMENTS OF BRANDING

BRAND NAME/BUSINESS NAME

The foundation of a business identity is its brand name, commonly referred to as its business name. It is the name that clients relate to a company, commodity, or service. A brand name must be carefully constructed, and while choosing a brand name, consideration for worldwide appeal must be given. You need to choose a name that will stick in people's minds. A business stands out from rivals with a distinctive and memorable name.

It makes the business more noticeable in a congested market, For instance, DANGOTE He had several areas of expertise, including salt, cement, sugar, etc., but his brand name remained the same for many years, helping him to become well-known. Although DANGOTE's items are made by other companies, he became well-known for his distinctive name.

Consider using "A.O Enterprise" instead of Adetula Olabisi Enterprises; it is short and distinctive, making it difficult for people to forget.

A business brand is frequently the first thing clients notice about it. It affects how they first see things and could make them more likely to continue interacting. A strong name effectively communicates crucial details about the company, such as its goals, core principles, or target market. It acts as a succinct means of expressing the brand's essence. A wise name choice also increases the effectiveness of marketing campaigns. A strong brand name makes it simpler to develop memorable slogans, logos, and commercials.

BUSINESS LOGO

A Business logo functions as a visual shorthand that quickly communicates its personality and mission, much like a brand's signature. It's an essential component of branding since it unites the business principles, goods, and services in a unified visual. A strong logo may be used on anything from business cards to billboards and yet be recognized and memorable. A logo establishes an emotional connection with clients via the use of colors, typefaces, and symbols, fostering loyalty and trust. It is a modest yet potent asset that has a significant impact on the identity and market image of a brand.

BUSINESS SLOGAN

Business slogans, often known as taglines or mottos, are brief expressions that capture a business corporate identity, core principles, or main products or services. They act as enduring hooks that make the brand and its USP more recognizable to customers. Well-written slogans have the power to stir feelings, convey a brand's promise, and set it apart from rivals. These succinct sayings are crucial to branding and marketing campaigns that want to make an impact on customers. The following is a list of a few company slogan examples:

- Able beads: "Beads with Class, makes a difference"
- Nike: "Just Do It"
- Apple: "Think Different"
- McDonald's: "I'm Lovin' It"
- Coca-Cola: "Open Happiness"
- FedEx: "When it Absolutely, Positively Has to Be There Overnight"
- Google: "Don't Be Evil"
- Toyota: "Let's Go Places"
- Wendy's: "Where's the Beef?"
- L'Oréal: "Because You're Worth It"

- Mastercard: "There are some things money can't buy. For everything else, there's Mastercard."

- McDonald's: "I'm Lovin' It"

- Microsoft: "Empower Every Person and Every Organization on the Planet to Achieve More"

Finally, develop a slogan for your business right away, dearie.

BUSINESS COLOR

Business colors have a significant impact on how consumers perceive a brand. Without using words, they convey qualities like trust, ingenuity, or dependability. Colors immediately conjure up associations, whether it's the calming blue of technological behemoths or the vivid red of fast-food franchises. Successful businesses use color psychology to evoke strong feelings in their

audience. From the logo and website to the packaging

and advertising, these colors are utilized throughout the

branding process. Businesses do this to create a visual

language that promotes loyalty and assists in recognition.

A strong weapon that goes beyond aesthetics, the choice

of company colors has a significant impact on how

organizations are viewed in a cutthroat marketplace.

Have a brand color for your business as a result, but

before choosing it, consider its significance and whether

it complements your business name.

PACKAGING

Business packaging involves more than just confinement; it's a calculated move. It includes the purposeful design, material choice, and presentation of items in order to communicate brand identity and shape customer views. A successful package approach improves product exposure, sets goods apart from those of rivals, and creates a positive consumer experience.

When creating packaging, businesses take into account elements including the target market, the product's features, and industry norms. Durability, safety, and environmental friendliness are all impacted by the material selection. Brands frequently aim for packaging that reflects their values, makes use of sustainable materials, and has minimal negative environmental effects.

Business packaging plays a part in effective logistics. Packaging that is well-designed guarantees that goods be carried securely and with less risk of harm. Effective packing dimensions may maximize storage space, resulting in cost savings and more efficient business processes.

E-commerce has increased the value of packaging throughout time. Unboxing experiences have evolved into social media material that affects how consumers perceive brands. Handwritten notes or imaginative designs are examples of personal touches that encourage consumer loyalty and word-of-mouth advertising.

Business packaging ultimately goes beyond a simple

functional requirement to become an essential

component of branding, client involvement, and

sustainable business practices.

CHAPTER 3

CRAFTING YOUR BRAND STORY

The Art of Storytelling in Business

A potent tool for branding, the art of storytelling enables businesses to engage their audience more deeply. Brands may effectively communicate their values, mission, and personality to consumers by using captivating storylines. In addition to advertising goods, good storytelling forges emotional connections and a feeling of authenticity.

Storytelling has the power to humanize a company and make it more relevant by creating believable people, interesting plotlines, and recounting the obstacles a brand has faced. It promotes brand loyalty and trust by assisting customers in comprehending the "why" behind a product.

In a congested market, narrative may also help a business stand out. Brands that stand out and leave a lasting impact on customers' thoughts are those that convey their stories in a distinctive and memorable way. This Increased brand awareness and customer retention may result from this. Ensuring that the storytelling adheres to the brand's identity and values is crucial. Authenticity is essential because customers can instantly tell when someone is trying to manipulate their feelings.

Every touchpoint, from commercials to social media,

should use the same well-crafted story to create a

consistent brand image. The goal of the art of

storytelling in branding is to build an emotional bond

between the target audience and the brand. It's a crucial

tool for businesses trying to stand out from the

competition, gain customer confidence, and develop

enduring partnerships.

Take "Nike" and its enduring "Just Do It" campaign as

an illustration.

The core theme of Nike's brand narrative is the pursuit of

excellence while pushing one's boundaries and

conquering obstacles. The story concentrates around the

journey of people who work hard to accomplish their

objectives in spite of the challenges they encounter. Athletes, regular individuals, or even imaginary characters that personify the spirit of tenacity and resiliency are frequently included in the stories. Nike uses its advertising campaigns to highlight not just their products but also the commitment and tenacity that the company represents.

Consider an advertisement with a young athlete who has failures and doubts but keeps training and becomes better. The story follows the athlete's journey through its highs and lows, recording moments of victory and weakness. The tale is in line with Nike's philosophy that everyone can succeed if they have the determination to "Just Do It."

Nike has been able to transcend its status as a sportswear manufacturer and transform into a symbol of inspiration and empowerment because to its narrative strategy. Numerous consumers have connected with the brand's recurring theme of pushing oneself and conquering obstacles, which has come to be associated with it.

In this approach, Nike's brand narrative forges an emotional bond with consumers, encouraging them to see their own potential and take initiative.

Aligning Your Values with Your Brand Story

There is more to developing a compelling brand values than merely telling a tale. Every facet of your brand's identity should reflect your basic principles. A true and enduring connection with your audience may be made when your principles and your story flow together naturally. Your company decisions are guided by this alignment, which also appeals to clients who have similar ideals. Never forget that a carefully created brand narrative based on principles may create brand differentiation in a crowded market, drive impact, and inspire loyalty.

5 Steps that will help you Align your Values to your Brand Story.

1. **Specify your core values:** Start by determining the core principles that guide your company. Think about the concepts that inform your choices and behavior. The identity of your brand will be built on these principles.

2. **Create a narrative structure:** Create a brand narrative that reflects your principles. Outline your story's main components, such as its beginning, goal, aim, and vision. Make sure your audience and your beliefs are reflected in your story.

3. **Integrate values into all touchpoints:** Embrace
    your ideals in all facets of the brand experience.
    Ensure consistency that represents your selected
    principles in everything you do, from your
    message and visual design to your customer
    interactions.

4. **Display Authenticity:** Your brand's behaviors
    should be consistent withits ideals. Be open and
    honest about how you're working to uphold these
    ideals in your company's operations and
    offerings. Authenticity improves the audience's
    sense of connection to your story.

5. **Engage and Change:** Discuss your ideals with
    your audience. Share examples of your adherence
    to these values in your stories, material, and
    projects. Be receptive to criticism and flexible

enough to adjust to shifting cultural and business

trends in order to ensure that your story holds up

over time.

CHAPTER 4

CREATING A SENSE OF TRUST AND CREDIBILITY

Presenting High Quality and Craftsmanship

Focus on demonstrating the meticulousness, accuracy, and top-notch materials utilized while exhibiting high quality and workmanship. Draw attention to the distinctive qualities that make the product stand out and the degree of skill and knowledge required to create it. To properly communicate the quality, use clear visuals like crisp photos or videos. Sharing the history of the product's production as well as the commitment of the craftsmen who worked on it may further boost its attractiveness. It takes careful planning to showcase the distinctive qualities and attraction of high quality, handcrafted items. Here's a how-to list in detail:

1 **Emphasize Unique Features:** Emphasize the stand-out characteristics that give the product its unique identity. This might be done through the use of unique design, hand-carved features, elaborate patterns, or rare materials.

2. **Focus on Details:** Zoom in on the exquisite craftsmanship. Take close-up pictures to show the accuracy and care that went into making the product.

3. **Display High-Quality Materials:** Describe the premium materials that were employed, highlighting their advantages and how they add to the product's total worth and sturdiness.

4. **Clear Product Description:** Give a succinct yet detailed overview of the product's features, advantages, and the user experience it delivers.

5. **Functionality Must Be Proven**: If the product demonstrates its functionality and how its excellent quality adds to a smooth user experience.

6. **Physical Demonstrations**: For physical items, think about holding live demonstrations, exhibits, or seminars

so that potential clients can see and handle the item in person.

7. **Utilize social media**: To publish aesthetically beautiful material that emphasizes craftsmanship. Examples of such platforms are Instagram, Pinterest, and YouTube. Engage with your audience and use relevant hashtags.

8. **Offer Customization**: If possible, provide customers the choice to customize. This not only demonstrates the adaptability of your skills but also enables clients to have a stronger connection to the final product.

9. **Transparency**: Be open and honest about the way products are made, emphasizing any ethical

considerations or use of environmentally friendly components. This may increase the attraction of the goods even further.

Do not forget that you want toMake an immersive experience that conveys the worth, excellence, and distinctiveness of your offering. To capture your audience and make a lasting impact, combine text, visual, and storytelling aspects.

Customers Review and Testimonials

Customer reviews are statements made by customers regarding their interactions with a brand, service, or company. Negative reviews can point out areas for development while positive evaluations can increase credibility, trust, and sales. As a business owner, you frequently have to read client evaluations and answer in order to interact with them and handle their issues.

Testimonials are declarations of approval or recommendation made by users who have had a good experience with a good or service. They often go into greater detail than evaluations and concentrate on certain advantages and results. Real names and images of consumers may be included. This might improve how credible testimonies are. Customer feedback and reviews are equally important in influencing public opinion and purchase choices.

Identifying And Comprehending Your Ideal Customers

The process of identifying and comprehending your ideal client requires determining the particular kind of individual or group that is most likely to profit from and use your product or service. This knowledge goes beyond simple demographics and explores people's interests, habits, problems, and goals. Gaining these insights will enable you to modify your marketing tactics, goods, and services to better meet their demands and forge a closer relationship, which will eventually improve client happiness and propel your organization forward. Finding and comprehending your ideal client demands constant effort and a blend of investigation, empathy, and adaptability. Your ability to service them and expand your firm is directly correlated to how well

you comprehend your consumers.

CHAPTER 5

EVOLVING YOUR BRAND OVER TIME

Making deliberate adjustments to various facets of your brand identity and strategy over time can help to keep it current, appealing, and in line with shifting customer tastes, market trends, and corporate objectives. The narrative, visual identity, product offers, and positioning of your brand may all need to be changed as part of this process.

Your brand will evolve as a result of your recognition of the cyclical nature of markets, consumer expectations, and trends. When you modify your brand, you can:

- *Maintain Relevance:* If a brand doesn't change, it may become out of date and lose its attractiveness to an evolving audience.

- *Gaining new demographics or target groups* that your present brand might not be appealing to might help you attract new customers.

- *Retain Current Clientele*: Careful brand adaptation may keep devoted clients from becoming alienated while also encouraging them to try something new.

- *Reflect Changes:* If your business has changed its emphasis, added new products to its line, or adopted new values, your brand should reflect those changes.

- *Effective competition* depends on your ability to differentiate yourself from rivals in a changing business environment.

- *Tell a Continual Story*: A brand's progress becomes a part of its story, showing its development and journey to customers.

- *Addressing cultural shifts* is possible through developing in response to societal and cultural developments that may affect brand perceptions.

- *Enhance Differentiation*: Brand evolution may help retain a unique selling offer as marketplaces grow crowded.

However, in order to retain continuity while accepting change, brand development should be properly planned and carried out. Instead of fully discarding your current brand, you should proactively update and refine it to ensure its success moving forward.

Refreshing Your Brand Elements Strategically

Refreshing brand elements strategically is a purposeful procedure that strives to give your brand new vitality while maintaining its core. To pinpoint opportunities for improvement, it requires assessing the competition environment, market trends, and consumer input. You may modernize visual components like your logo and colors to represent your brand's beliefs and goals if you have a firm knowledge of them.

Furthermore, fine-tuning your messaging and tone guarantees that your brand's voice stays current and connects with your audience. To keep devoted customers connected to your brand and able to identify it, it's critical to find a balance between innovation and familiarity. You may deliberately update your brand's aspects to position it for development, draw in new consumers, and show your brand's flexibility and relevance in a variety of contexts in the marketplace.

Measuring Brand Success

The efficacy and influence of your brand on your target audience and the market as a whole are measured using a variety of indicators. Key performance indicators include the following:

1. **Brand Awareness**: Measuring how well-known your brand is to your target market.

2. **Brand equity:** Analyzing how customers evaluate the worth and repute of your brand.

3. **Measuring consumer loyalty**: how frequently and persistently customers select your brand over rivals.

4. **Customer Engagement**: Examining the degree of online and offline customer engagement and contact with your business.

5. **Sales and Revenue**: Tracking how your brand affects the growth of your sales and revenue.

6. **Social Media Metrics:** Measuring the increase of followers on social media and the number of likes, shares, comments, and likes.

7. **Understanding** how effectively your brand satisfies client expectations by gathering feedback and reviews.

8. **Understanding** how your brand is seen in terms of attributes, ideals, and associations by conducting surveys or focus groups.

9. **Brand Consistency**: Making sure that all of your brand's aspects are consistent.

You may get information about your brand's performance, spot opportunities for development, and make wise choices to increase brand success over time by monitoring these aspects.

CONCLUSION

YOUR NEXT STEP IN BRANDING YOUR HANDMADE BUSINESS

Consider developing a distinctive Brand Name, logo, outlining your business principles and stories, interacting with your audience on social media, and exhibiting your creative process through behind-the-scenes material to further brand your handmade business. To boost your awareness, look at packaging alternatives that complement the aesthetics of your business, collaborate with influencers, and take part in regional events.

www.ingramcontent.com/pod-product-compliance
Lightning Source LLC
Chambersburg PA
CBHW051358250726
48656CB00006B/2154